MYSTICISM OF SOUND

MYSTICISM OF SOUND

Inayat Khan

PILGRIMS PUBLISHING
Varanasi•Kathmandu

MYSTICISM OF SOUND

By Inayat Khan

Published by
PILGRIMS PUBLISHING

An imprint of
PILGRIMS BOOK HOUSE
B 27/98 A-8, Nawabganj Road
Durga Kund
Varanasi, India 221010
Tel: 91-542-314060, 312496
Fax: 91-542-314059
E-mail: pilgrims@satyam.net.in

Distributed in India by
BOOK FAITH INDIA
414-416 Express Tower
Azadpur Commercial Complex
New Delhi-110033, India
Tel: 91-11-713-2459
Fax: 91-11-724-9674
E-mail: pilgrim@del2.vsnl.net.in

Distributed in Nepal by
PILGRIMS BOOK HOUSE
P.O Box 3872
Kathmandu, Nepal
Tel: 977-1-424942
Fax: 977-1-424943
E-mail: pilgrims@wlink.com.np

First published in London in 1923

Edited by C.N. Burchett
Layout by Hom KC

Cover design by Sasya

Printed in India

Contents

Introduction

Music is one of man's most ancient forms of entertainment. Music in its different forms has found its reference in the most ancient of scriptures world wide. It was no doubt the most basic form in which man could express his emotions and feelings towards his environment and his fellow men.

It has been found that man's likes and dislikes with regard to musical form are very relevant to the note of vibration with which his body is attuned. Taking into consideration the states of evolution of man, for example Angelic, Human, Animal or Devilish, this factor plays a very big part in this process. Earthy music produces movement and activity in the body, whereas water produces a vibration which induces a dream like state which is taken over by one's imagination thus leading one into an imaginary environment. Fire on the other hand induces fear while air is found to be more powerful than all the others put together and creates a feeling of ecstasy.

I

The Sufis paid a great deal of attention to the harmonious and rhythmic use of language and thus brought the use of music into their daily devotions and meditation making it a tool of their practices. The use of sound has always played a great role in religious practices.

Once one goes more deeply into the origins and reasons for music it can be seen that in fact music may have itself been the beginning of language and it is only as we have simplified our language to suit our needs that it has moved away from the harmony and rhythm of music. In this book the author has laid out in very simple terms the relation between music and mysticism. It becomes even clearer as he reveals the mystic charms that music has held for man since creation. So deeply are our souls moved by music that skillful and creative musicians can reduce us to tears or lift us up to unimaginable heights simply with their deft use of harmonies and tones at their disposal.

Music may produce the moods or create the environment that are required for any particular occasion. Highly popular and competent musicians often play music to satisfy the needs of their audience and often determine their moods before they present their program. This, one might add, is no less a skill than being a competent musician

Musical soirees very popular in 18th and 19th century Europe provided the entertainment for the upper classes, whilst folk dances and folk music were the forte of the working class. Each form having its own intellectual levels to suit its audience. Today all kinds of music are available to each and everyone of us, but still it is seen that each person makes his own choice according to his intellect and particular likings. All this goes to prove the seers right that each man has his own vibration which is satisfied by a particular form of music.

I

The Silent Life

The Life Absolute from which has sprung all that is felt, seen, and perceived, and into which all in time again merges, is a silent, motionless and eternal life which among the Sufis is called Zat. Every motion that springs forth from this silent life is a vibration and a creator of vibrations. Within one vibration are created many vibrations; as motion causes motion so the silent life becomes active in a certain part, and creates every moment more and more activity, losing thereby the peace of the original silent life. It is the grade of activity of these vibrations that accounts for the various planes of existence. These planes are imagined to differ from one another, but in reality they cannot be entirely detached and made separate from one another. The activity of vibrations makes them grosser, and thus the earth is born of the heavens.

The mineral, vegetable, animal and human kingdoms are the gradual changes of vibrations, and the vibrations of each plane differ from one another in their weight, breadth, length, color, effect, sound and rhythm. Man is not only formed of vibrations, but he lives and moves in them; they surround him as the fish is surrounded by water, and he contains them within him as the tank contains water. His different moods, inclinations, affairs, successes and failures, and all conditions of life depend upon a certain activity of vibrations, whether these be thoughts, emotions or feelings. It is the direction of the activity of vibrations that accounts for the variety of things and beings. This vibratory activity is the basis of sensation, and the source of all pleasure and pain; its cessation, is the opposite, of sensation. All sensations, are caused, by a certain grade, of activity of vibration.

There are two aspects of vibrations; fine and gross; both, containing, varied degrees. Some are perceived by the soul, some by the mind, and some by the eyes. What the soul perceives are of the feelings; what the mind conceives of are the thoughts; what the eyes see are the vibrations solidified from their ethereal state, and turned into atoms, which appear in the physical world, constituting the elements; ether, air, fire, water and earth. The

2

finest vibrations are imperceptible even to the soul. The soul itself, is formed of these vibrations; it is their activity, which makes it conscious.

Creation begins with the activity of consciousness, which may be called vibration, and every vibration starting from its original source is the same, differing only in its tone and rhythm caused by a greater or lesser degree of force behind it. In the plane of sound, vibration causes diversity of tone, and in the world of atoms, diversity of color. It is by massing together that the vibrations become audible, but at each step towards the surface they multiply, and as they advance they materialize. Sound gives to the consciousness an evidence of its existence, although it is in fact the active part of consciousness itself which turns into sound. The knower so to say becomes known to himself, in other words the consciousness bears witness to its own voice. It is therefore that sound appeals to man. All things being derived from and formed of vibrations have sound hidden within them, as fire in flint; and each atom of the universe confesses by its tone "My sole origin is but sound." If any solid or sonorous body is struck it will answer back, "I am sound."

Sound has its birth, death, sex, form, planet, god, color, childhood, youth and age, but that volume of sound which is in the abstract beyond the sphere of the concrete is the origin and basis of all sound.

Both sound and color make their effect on the human soul according to the law of harmony; to a fine soul color appeals, and to a still finer soul sound. Tone has either a warm or a cold effect, according to its element, since all elements are made of different degrees of vibrations. Therefore sound can produce an agreeable or a disagreeable effect upon man's mind and body, and has its healing effect in the absence of herbs and drugs which also have their origin in vibrations.

Manifestations being formed of vibrations, the planets are the primal manifestations, each planet having its peculiar tone; therefore every note represents one planet. Every individual therefore has a note peculiar to himself which is according to his birth planet; for this reason a certain tone appeals to a particular person according to the grade of his evolution. Every element has a sound peculiar to itself; in the finer element the circle of sound expands, and in the grosser element it narrows. It is therefore distinct in the former and indistinct in the latter.

The earth has various aspects of beauty as well as of variety in its sound. Its pitch is on the surface, its form is crescent-like, and its color is yellow. The sound of earth is dim and dull, and produces a thrill, activity and movement in the body. All instruments of wire and gut, as well as the instruments of percussion, such as the drum, cymbals, etc., represent the sound of the earth.

4

The sound of water is deep, its form is serpentlike, its color green, and it is best heard in the roaring of the sea. The sound of running water, of mountain rills, the drizzling and pattering of rain, the sound of water running from a pitcher into a jar, from a pipe into a tub, from a bottle into a glass, all have a smooth and lively effect, and a tendency to produce imagination, whim, dream, affection, and emotion. The instrument called "Jalatarang" is an arrangement of china bowls or glasses graduated in size and filled with water in proportion to the desired scale, more water lowers the tone, and less raises it. These instruments have a touching effect upon the emotions of the heart.

The sound of fire is high pitched, its form is curled, and its color red. It is heard in the falling of the thunderbolt and in a volcanic eruption, in the sound of a fire when blazing, in the noise of squibs, crackers, rifles, guns and cannons. All these have a tendency to produce fear.

The sound of air is wavering, its form zig-zag, and its color blue. Its voice is heard in storms, when the wind blows, and in the whisper of the morning breeze. Its effect is breaking, sweeping and piercing. The sound of air finds expression in all wind instruments made of wood, brass, and bamboo, it has a tendency to kindle the fire of the heart, as Rumi writes in his Masnevi about the flute.

Krishna is always portrayed in Indian art with a flute. The air-sound overpowers all other sounds, for it is living, and in its every aspect its influence produces ecstasy.

The sound of ether is self-contained, and it holds all forms and colors. It is the base of all sounds; and is the undertone which is ever continuous.

Its instrument is the human body, because it can be audible through it; although it is all pervading, yet it is unheard. It manifests to man as he purifies his body from material properties The body can become its proper instrument when the space within is opened, when all the tubes and veins in it are free. Then the sound which exists externally in space becomes manifest inwardly also Ecstacy, illumination, restfulness, fearlessness, rapture, joy, and revelation are the effects of this sound. To some it manifests of itself, to others when they are in a negative state caused by weakness of the body or mind; to neither of these is it a benefit, but on the other hand it causes them to become abnormal. This sound only elevates those who open themselves to it by the sacred practices known to the Mystics.

The sound of earth and water commingled has tenderness and delicacy. The sound of earth and air has strength and power. The sound of water and fire has a lively and animating effect. The sound of water with

6

ether has a soothing and comforting effect. The sound of fire and air has a terrifying and fearsome effect. The sound of fire with ether has a breaking and freeing effect. The sound of air with ether produces calm and peace.

II

Vibrations

The silent life experiences on the surface by reason of activity. The silent life appears as death in comparison with the life of activity on the surface. Only to the wise the life eternal seems preferable on account of the ever-changing and momentary nature of mortal life. The life on the surface seems to be the real life, because it is in this life that all joy is experienced.

In the silent life there is no joy but only peace. The Soul's original being is peace and its nature is joy, both of which work against each other. This is the hidden cause of all life's tragedy. The soul originally is without any experience, it experiences all when it opens its eyes to the exterior plane, and keeps them open, enjoying the life on the surface until satisfied. The soul then begins to close its eyes to the exterior plane, and constantly seeks peace, the original state of its being.

The inward and essential part of each and every being is composed of fine vibrations, and the external part is formed of the gross.

The finer part we name spirit and the grosser matter; the former being less subject to change and destruction and the latter more so. All that lives is spirit and all that dies is matter; and all that dies in spirit is matter and all that lives in matter is spirit. All that is visible and perceptible appears to be living, although subject to death and decay, and becoming every moment resolved into its finer element; but the sight of man is so deluded on account of its wakefulness to the seeming world that the spirit really lives, is covered under the garb of matter and its true being is hidden. It is the gradually increasing activity which causes vibrations to materialize, and it is the gradual decrease of the same which transmutes them again into spirit. As has been said, vibrations pass through five distinct phases while changing from the fine to the gross; and the elements of ether, air, fire, water and earth each has a savor, color, and form peculiar to itself. This wheel of elements brings them all in time to the surface. At each step in their activity they vary and become distinct from each other; and it is the grouping of these vibrations which causes variety in the objective world. The law which causes them to disperse man calls destruction.

Vibrations turn to atoms and atoms generate what we call life; thus it happens that their grouping by the power of nature's affinity forms a living entity; and as the breath manifests through the form so the body becomes conscious. In one individual there are many fine and small beings hidden; in his blood, in his brain cells, in his skin, and in all planes of his existence. As in the physical being of an individual many small germs are being born and nourished which are nevertheless living beings, so in his mental plane also there are many beings, termed Mawakals, the elementals; and these are still finer entities born of man's own thoughts, and as the germs live in his physical body so the elementals dwell in his mental sphere. Man often imagines that thoughts are without life; he does not see that they are more alive than the physical germs and that they have a birth, childhood, youth, age and death, they work for man's advantage or disadvantage according to their nature. The Sufi creates, fashions and controls them. He drills them and rules them throughout his life, they form his army and carry out his desires. As the germs constitute man's physical being and the elementals his mental life, so do the Angels constitute his spiritual existence.

Vibrations as a rule have their length as well as breadth; they may last the least fraction of a moment or the greater part of the age of the universe. They make different forms, figures, and colors, as they shoot forth, one vibration creating another, and thus myriads arise out of one. In this way there are circles under circles and circles over circles, all of which form the universe. Every vibration after its manifestation becomes merged again in its original source. The reach of vibrations is according to the fineness of the plane of their starting point. To speak more plainly, the word uttered by the lips can only reach the ears of the hearer; but the thought proceeding from the mind reaches far, shooting from mind to mind. The vibrations of mind are much stronger than those of words. The earnest feelings of one heart can pierce the heart of another, they speak in the silence, spreading out into the sphere, so that the very atmosphere of a person's presence proclaims his thoughts and emotions, The vibrations of the soul are the most powerful and far-reaching they run as an electric current from soul to soul.

All things and beings in the universe are connected with each other, visibly or invisibly, and through vibrations a communication is established between them, in all the planes of existence; as an ordinary instance, if one person coughs in an assembly, many others begin to do the same, and the same is the case with yawning. This also applies to laughter, excitement and depression. This shows that vibrations convey the conditions of one being to another, therefore the Seer knows of the past, present and future, and perceives conditions on all planes of existence.

Vibrations work through the cord of sympathy existing between man and his surroundings and reveal the past, present and future conditions; this explains why the howling of dogs foretells death, and the neighing of horses the approach of danger. Not only animals show this but even the plants in times of sorrow begin to die, and the flowers to fade, while during times of happiness they grow and flourish. The reason why the plants and animals can perceive the vibrations and know of coming events while man is ignorant of them, is because he has blinded himself with egotism. The influence of vibrations is left on the chair on which one sits, in the bed where one has slept, in the house where one lives, in the clothes one wears, in the food one eats, and even in the street where one walks.

Every emotion arises from the intensity of the activity of vibrations, which when active in different directions produce different emotions; the main cause of every emotion being activity alone. Every vibration while active raises the consciousness to the outermost surface, and the mist caused by this activity collects clouds which we call emotions. The clouds of emotion obscure the clear sight of the soul. Therefore passion is called blind. The excess of the activity of vibrations not only blinds, but weakens the will, and a weak will enfeebles the mind and body.

It is the state of vibrations to which man is tuned that accounts for his soul's note. The different degrees of these notes form a variety of pitch divided by the Mystics into three distinct grades. First, the grade which produces power and intelligence, and may be pictured as a calm sea. Secondly, the grade of moderate activity which keeps all things in motion, and is a balance between power and weakness which may be pictured as the sea in motion. Thirdly the grade of intense activity, which destroys everything and causes all weakness and blindness; which may be pictured as a stormy sea.

In the activity of all things and beings the pitch is recognized by the *Seer*, as a musician knows the *Key* in which any particular music is written. Man's atmosphere tells of the grade of activity of his vibrations.

If vibratory activity is properly controlled, man may experience all life's joy, and at the same time not be enslaved by it. It is most difficult to control activity when it is once started and on the increase, for it is like trying to control a runaway horse. But yet in the control abides the whole of what is called mastership.

The Saints and Sages spread their peace not only in the place where they sit, but even in the neighborhood where they dwell; the town, or the country, where they live is at peace, in accordance with the power of vibrations they send out form their soul. This is the reason why association with good or bad and with those of the upper or lower classes has a great influence upon the life and character of man. The vibrations of thought and feeling create, procure, and prepare of themselves all the necessary means for their manifestation on the surface. For example a person may desire to eat fish and instead of ordering it might think strongly of it, his thought vibrations thus speaking to the mental ears of the cook, give him the same desire and perhaps his strong feeling would even attract a fishmonger to the house. In this way the thoughts of Sages work out their destiny, according to the strength, power and purity of their minds. A certain degree of thought-power is needed to bring about a certain result; as so much dynamite is required to blast a single rock and an infinitely greater quantity is necessary to make a tunnel through a mountain.

The length of time that the thought is held has also much to do with its accomplishment, for the thought vibrations have to be active for a certain time to bring about a certain result. A certain length of time is required for the baking of a cake, if it is hurried the cake will be uncooked, by too great a heat it will burn. If the operator of the mental vibrations lacks patience then the power of thought will be waste, even if it were half way to its destiny; or still nearer to a successful issue. If too great a power of thought is given to the accomplishment of a certain thing it destroys while preparing it.

In order to reflect thought and feeling on another, man should observe the same rule as in voice and word. The louder a person speaks in an assembly the more attention he attracts and all those present perforce give him a hearing. In the same way if a Sufi sends the vibrations of his thought and feeling, they naturally strike with a great strength and power on any mind on which they happen to fall. As sweetness of voice has a winning power so it is with tenderness of thought and feeling. Thought-vibrations to which the spoken word is added are doubled in strength and with a physical effort this strength is trebled. Reason is like fire, it gives light to the thought but thought overheated loses its power, as heat can weaken the physical body. Reason gives birth to doubt which destroys thought-power before it is able to fulfil its destiny. The strength of thought-power consists in confidence or faith. Reason confuses, and doubts scatter the waves of thought-vibrations, which disperse and go off in different directions from lack of the strength that binds. One should never think or speak against one's desire, for it weakens the thought-vibration and often brings about contrary results. A variety of thoughts

15

springing up at the same time. naturally
enfeebles the power of mind, for none of them
have a chance to mature, just as twins are as
a rule imperfect and triplets seldom live. The
disharmony between one's desire and one's
ideal always causes a great confusion in life
for they constantly work against each other.
When a person speaks, thinks, or feels either
hardly or kindly of another, it reaches the
spirit of that one either consciously or
unconsciously by the power of vibration. If we
happen to be offended with someone and do
not give it out in speech or action, it cannot be
hidden, for the vibrations of our feeling will
reach directly to the person in question, and
he will begin to feel our displeasure, however
far away he may be. The same is the case with
our love and pleasure, however we may try to
conceal it in speech or action it cannot be
hidden. This explains the old adage that even
the wall is not impervious to vibrations of
thought.

Sufis give special attention to the good and
bad wishes of people. They strive continually
to attract the good wishes of others whether
worthy or unworthy, by every means in their
power. The intensity of activity produces
strong vibrations named in Sufic terms Jelal;
the gentleness of activity causes mild
vibrations called Jemal. The former activity
works as strength and power, the latter as
beauty and grace. The conflict of both these

forces is termed Kemal, and causes nothing but destruction.

The standard of right and wrong, the conception of good and evil, and the idea of sin and virtue are understood differently by the people of different races, nations, and religions, therefore it is difficult to discern the law governing these opposites. It becomes clear however by understanding the law of vibrations. Every thing and being on the surface of existence seem separate from one another, but in every plane beneath the surface they approach nearer to each other, and in the innermost plane they all become one. Every disturbance therefore caused to the peace of the smallest part of existence on the surface, inwardly affects the whole. Thus any thought, speech and action that disturbs peace is wrong, evil, and a sin; if it brings about peace it is right, good, and a virtue. Life being as a dome, its nature is also dome-like. Disturbance of the slightest part of life disturbs the whole and returns as a curse upon the person who caused it; any peace produced on the surface comforts the whole, and thence returns as peace to the producer.

This is the philosophy of the reward of good deeds and the punishment of bad deeds given by the Higher Powers.

III

Harmony

Harmony is the source of manifestation, the cause of its existence, and the medium between God and man.

The peace for which every soul strives, and which is the true nature of God, and the utmost goal of man, is but the outcome of harmony; this shows that all life's attainments without a sense of harmony are but vain. It is the attainment of harmony which is called Heaven, and it is the lack of it which is termed Hell. The master of it alone understands life, and he who lacks it is foolish in spite of all other knowledge that he may have acquired.

The Sufi gives great importance to the attainment of harmony, believing that light is for angels and darkness for the devil, but that harmony is necessary for a human being in order to keep a balance in life.

There are three aspects of harmony: (I) Eternal, (2) Universal, and (3) Individual.

Eternal Harmony is the harmony of consciousness, which being in itself eternal, all things and beings live and move in it, yet it remains remote, undisturbed, and peaceful. This is the God of the believer, and the God of the knower, all vibrations from the finest to the grossest are held together by this harmony, as well as each atom of manifestation, and both creation and destruction take place in order to uphold it. Its power eventually attracts each being towards the Everlasting peace.

Man is drawn in two opposite directions by the power of harmony, towards the Infinite and towards Manifestation, and he is less conscious of the former than of the latter, and by facing towards the one direction he loses sight of the other.

The Infinite, being the essential spirit of all, finally attracts all to itself. The Sufi gives most importance to harmony with the Infinite, which he realizes by resignation to the will of God, the Beloved.

The existence of land and water, the land for the water, and the water for the land; the attraction between the heavens and the earth, all demonstrate a universal harmony. The attraction of the sun and moon to each other, the cosmic order of the stars and the planets, all connected and related with each other, moving and working under a certain law; the regular rotation of the seasons, the night following the day, and the day in its giving place to the night; the dependence of one being on another, the distinctiveness, attraction and assimilation of the five elements, all prove the universal harmony.

The male and female, beast and bird, vegetable and rock, and all classes of things and beings are linked together and attracted to each other with a cord of harmony. If one being or thing however apparently useless were missing in this universe of endless variety, it would be as it were a note missing in a song. "Every being is born for a certain purpose, and the light of that purpose is kindled within his soul." *Saadi*.

All famines, plagues, and disasters such as storms, floods, volcanic eruptions, wars and revolutions, however bad they may appear to man, are in reality for the adjusting of this universal harmony.

There is a story told in India of how once all the inhabitants of a village which had suffered from drought, gathered together before the Temple of their God praying that for this year an abundance of rain might fall.

A voice from the Unseen replied: "Whatever We do is for the betterment of Our purpose, ye have no right to interfere with Our work, oh! Ye men."

But they again cried for mercy, and continued to do so more persistently. Then came the answer saying: "Your prayers, fastings, and sacrifices have induced Us to grant for this one year as much rain as ye desire." They all returned home rejoicing. In the autumn they worked vigorously on their farms, and after having prepared the ground and sown the seed, they prayed for rain. When they considered that sufficient had fallen they again had recourse to prayer, and the rain ceased. In this way an ideal crop of corn was produced, and all the inhabitants of that country made merry over it. This year more corn was grown than ever before. After the crops were gathered in however, all those who ate the corn died and many were the victims. In perplexity they again sought the God bowing low before the Temple crying: "Why hast Thou shown such wrath to us, after having shown so great a mercy? The God replied: "It was not Our wrath, but your folly for interfering with Our Work; We sometimes send a drought, and at other times a flood, so that a portion of your crops may be destroyed, but We have Our reasons for so doing for in this way, all that is poisonous and undesirable in them is also destroyed, leaving only what is beneficial for the preservation of your life." The villagers prostrated themselves in humble prayer saying: "We shall never again try to control the affairs of the universe, Thou art the Creator and Thou art the Controller, we are thine innocent children, and Thou alone knowest what is best for us." The Creator knows how to control His world, what to bring and what to destroy.

There are two aspects of individual harmony (1) the harmony between body and soul, (2) the harmony between individuals.

The soul rejoices in the comforts experienced by the external self, yet man becomes so engrossed in them that the soul's true comfort is neglected, and this keeps man dissatisfied through all the momentary comforts he may enjoy, but not understanding this, he attributes the cause of his dissatisfaction to some unsatisfied desire in his life. The outlet of all earthly passions gives a momentary satisfaction, yet creates a tendency for more; in this struggle the satisfaction of the soul is overlooked by man who is constantly busied in the pursuit of his earthly enjoyment and comfort, depriving the soul of its true bliss. The true delight of the soul lies in love, harmony, and beauty, the outcome of which are wisdom, calm, and peace, the more constant they are the greater is the satisfaction of the soul.

If man in his daily life would examine every action which has reflected a disagreeable picture of himself upon his soul and caused a darkness and dissatisfaction, and if on the other hand he would consciously watch each thought, word, or deed which had produced an inward love, harmony and beauty, and each feeling which had brought him wisdom, calm, and peace, then the way of harmony between soul and body would be easily understood, and both aspects of life would be satisfied, the inner as well as the outer. The soul's satisfaction is much more important than that of the body, for it is more lasting. In this way the thought, speech, and action can be adjusted so that harmony may be established first in the self by the attunement of body and soul.

The next aspect of individual harmony is practised in one's contact with another. Every being has an individual Ego produced from his own illusion. This limits his view which is led in the direction of his own interest, and he judges of good and bad, high or low, right or wrong in relation to himself and others, through his limited view, which is generally partial and imaginary rather than true. This darkness is caused by the overshadowing of the soul by the external self. Thus a person becomes blind to his own infirmities as well as to the merits of another, and the right action of another becomes wrong in his eyes and the fault of the self seems right. This is the case with mankind in general, until the veil of darkness is lifted from his eyes.

The *nufs*, the Ego of an individual, causes all disharmony with the self as well as with others, thus showing its unruliness in all aspects of life. The lion, the sovereign among all animals, most powerful and majestic, is always unwelcome to the inhabitants of the forest, and he is even unfriendly to his own kind. Two lions will never greet one another in a friendly way, for their nufs is so strong; and although the lion the ruler of all other animals, he is a slave to his own passions which make his life restless. The *nufs* of herbivorous animals such as the sheep and goat is subdued, for this reason they are harmless to one another, and are on the contrary harmonious enough to live in herds. The harmony and sympathy existing among them makes them mutually partake of their joys and sorrows; but they easily fall a victim to the wild animals of the forest.

The Masters of the past like Moses and Mohamed have always loved to tend their flocks in the jungles and Jesus Christ spoke of himself as the Good Shepherd, while St. John the Baptist spoke of the Lamb of God, harmless, and innocent, ready for sacrifice.

The nufs of the bird is still milder, therefore upon one tree many and various kinds can live as one family, singing the praise of God in unison, and flying about in flocks of thousands.

Among birds are to be found those who recognize their mate and who live together, harmoniously building the nest for their young, each in turn sitting on the eggs, and bearing their part in the upbringing of their little ones. Many times they mourn and lament over the death of their mate. The *nufs* of the insects is still less, they walk over each other without doing any harm, and live together in millions, as one family, without distinction of friend or foe. This proves how the power of nufs grows at each step in nature's evolution, and culminates in man, creating disharmony all through his life, unless it is subdued, producing thereby a calm and peace within the self, and a sense of harmony with others. Every human being has an attribute peculiar to his *nufs*. One is tiger-like, another resembles a dog, while a third may be like a cat and a fourth like a fox. In this way man shows in his speech, thoughts and feelings the beasts and birds, and the condition of his *nufs* is akin to their nature, and at times his very appearance resembles them. Therefore his tendency to harmony depends upon the evolution of his *nufs*.

As man begins to see clearly through human life, the world begins to appear as a forest to him, filled with wild animals, fighting, killing, and preying upon one another.

There are four different classes of men who harmonize with each other in accordance with their different states of evolution. They are (1) Angelic; (2) Human; (3) Animal; (4) Devilish.

The angelic seeks for heaven, and the human being struggles along in the world, the man with animal propensities revels in his earthly pleasures, while the devilish man is engaged in creating mischief, thereby making a hell for himself and for others. Man after his human evolution becomes angelic, and through his development in animality arrives at the stage of devil.

In music the law of harmony is that the nearest note does not make a consonant interval. This explains the prohibition of marriage between close relatives because of their nearness in merit and blood. As a rule harmony lies in contrast. Men fight with men and women quarrel with women, but the male and the female are as a rule harmonious to each other and a complete oneness makes a perfect harmony. In every being the five elements are constantly working, and in every individual, one, especially predominates. The wise have therefore distinguished five different natures in man, according to the element predominant in him. Sometimes two elements or even more predominate in a human being to a greater or lesser degree.

The harmony of life can be learnt in the same way as the harmony of music. The ear should be trained to distinguish both tone and word, and the meaning concealed within, and to know from the verbal meaning and the tone of voice whether it is a true word or a false note; to distinguish between sarcasm and sincerity, between words spoken in jest, and those spoken in earnest, to understand the difference between true admiration and flattery, to distinguish true admiration and flattery, to distinguish modesty from humility, a smile from a sneer, arrogance from pride, either directly or indirectly expressed. By so doing the ear becomes gradually trained in the same way as in music, and a word as well as those of another are false or true. Man should learn in what tone to express a certain thought or feeling as in voice cultivation. There are times when he should speak loudly, and there are times when a soft tone of voice is needed, for every word a certain note, and for every speech a certain pitch is necessary. At the same time there should be a proper use of a natural, sharp or flat notes as well as a consideration of key.

There are nine different aspects of feeling, each of which has a certain mode of expression.

(1) Mirth, expressed in a lively tone.
(2) Grief, expressed in a pathetic tone.
(3) Fear in a broken voice.
(4) Mercy in a tender voice.
(5) Wonder in an exclamatory tone.
(6) Courage in an emphatic tone.
(7) Frivolity, in a light tone.
(8) Attachment, in a deep tone.
(9) Indifference, in the voice of silence.

An untrained person confuses these. He whispers the words which should be known and speaks out loudly those which should be hidden. A certain subject must be spoken in a high pitch, while another requires a lower pitch. One should consider the place, the number of persons present, the kind of people and their evolution, and speak in accordance with the understanding of others, as it is said, "Speak to people in their own language." With a child one must have childish talk, with the young only suitable words should be spoken, with the old speak in accordance with their understanding. In the same way there should be a graduated way of expressing our thought so that every body may not be driven with the same whip. It is the consideration for others which distinguishes man from the animals. It must be understood that rhythm is the balance of speech and action. One must speak at the right time, otherwise silence is better than speech. A word of sympathy with the grief of another, and should watch the opportunity for moving a subject of conversation, but skilfully blend two subjects with a harmonious link. Also one should wait patiently while another speaks, and keep a rein on the speech when the thought rushes out uncontrollably, in order to keep it in rhythm and under control during its outlet. One should emphasize the important words with a consideration of strong and weak accent. It is necessary to choose the right word and mode of expression, to regulate the speed and to know how to keep the rhythm. Some people begin to speak slowly and gradually increase the speed to such an extent that they are unable to speak coherently. The above-named rules apply to all actions in life.

The Sufi like student of music trains both his voice and ear in the harmony of life. The training of the voice consists in being conscientious about each word spoken, of its tone, rhythm, meaning and the appropriateness for the occasion. For instance, the words of consolation should be spoken in a slow rhythm, with a soft voice and sympathetic tone. When speaking words of command a lively rhythm is necessary, and a powerful and distinct voice. The Sufi avoids all unrhythmic actions; he keeps the rhythm of his speech under the control of patience, not speaking a word before the right time, not giving an answer until the question is finished. A contradictory word he considers a discord unless spoken in a debate, and even at such times he tries to resolve it into a consonant chord. A contradictory tendency in man finally develops into a passion until he contradicts even his own idea if it be propounded by another. The Sufi in order to keep harmony even modulates his speech from one key to another, in other words he falls in with another person's idea by looking at the subject from the speaker's point of view instead of his own. He makes a base for every conversation with an appropriate introduction, thus preparing the ears of the listener for a perfect response. He watches his every movement and expression, as well as those of others, trying to form a consonant chord of harmony between himself and another. The attainment of harmony in life takes a longer time to acquire and a more careful study than does the training of the ear and the cultivation of the voice, although it is acquired in the same manner as the knowledge of music. To the ear of the Sufi every word spoken is like a note which is true when harmonious, and false when inharmonious. He makes the scale of his speech either major, minor, or chromatic as occasion demands, and his words either sharp, flat, or natural are in accord with the law of harmony. For instance the straight, polite and tactful manner of speech is as his major, minor, or chromatic scale, representing dominance, respect, and equality. He takes a similar arbitrary or contrary motion to suit the time and situation by following step by step, by agreeing and differing and even by opposing and yet keeping up the law of harmony in conversation. Take any two persons as two notes, the harmony existing between them forms intervals either consonant or dissonant, perfect or imperfect, major or minor, diminished or augmented as the two persons may be. The interval of class, creed, cast, race, nation or religion, as well as the interval of age, or state of evolution, or of varied and opposite interests shows the law here distinctly. A wise man would be more likely in harmony with his foolish servant than with a semi-wise man who considers himself infallible. Again it is equally possible that a wise man may be far from happy in the society of the foolish, and vice versa. The proud man will always quarrel with the proud while he will support the humble. It is also possible for the proud to agree on a common question of pride, such as pride of race or birth. Sometimes the interval between the disconnected notes is filled by a middle note forming a consonant chord. For instance the discord between husband and wife may be removed by the link of a child, or the discord between brothers and sisters may be taken away by the intervention of the mother or father. In this way, however inharmonious two persons may be, the forming of a consonant chord by an intervening link creates harmony. A foolish person is pliable. The former sticks to his ideas, likes, dislikes, and convictions whether right or wrong, while the latter makes them sharp or flat by raising or lowering the tone and pitch, harmonizing with the other as the occasion demands. The key it has all notes of the scale within it. In the same way the Sufi harmonizes with everybody whether good or bad, wise or foolish, by becoming as the key note.

All races, nations, classes and people are like a strain of music based upon one chord, when the keynote, the common interest, holds so many personalities in a single bond of harmony. By a study of life the Sufi learns and practises the nature of its harmony. He establishes harmony with the self, with others, with the Universe and with the Infinite. He identifies with another, he sees himself, so to say, in every other being. He cares of neither blame nor praise considering both as coming from himself. If a person were to drop a heavy weight and in so doing hurt his own foot, he would not blame his hand for having dropped it, realizing himself in both the hand and the foot. In like manner the Sufi is tolerant when harmed by another, thinking that the harm has come from himself alone. He uses counterpoint by blending the undesirable talk of the friend making it into a fugue.

He overlooks the faults of others, considering that they know no better. He hides the faults of others, and suppresses any facts that would cause in harmony. His constant fight is with the *nufs*, the root of all disharmony and the only enemy of man. By crushing this enemy man gains mastery over self; this wins for him mastery over the whole universe, because the wall standing between the self and the Almighty has been broken down. Gentleness, mildness, respect, humility, modesty, self-denial, conscientiousness, tolerance and forgiveness are considered by the Sufi as the attributes which produce harmony within one's own soul as well as within that of another. Arrogance, wrath, vice, attachment, greed and jealousy are the six principal sources of disharmony. *Nufs*, the only creator or disharmony, the more it is pleased. For the time being it shows its satisfaction at having gratified its demands, but soon after demands still more, until life becomes a burden, The wise detect this enemy as the instigator of all mischief, but everybody else blames another for his misfortunes in life.

IV

Name

The variety of things and beings and the peculiarities which make them differ cause the necessity of name. Name produces the picture of a form, figure, color, size, quality, quantity, feeling and sense of things and beings, not only perceptible, and comprehensible, but even of those beyond perception and comprehension, therefore its importance is greater than all things. There is a great secret hidden in a name, be it the name of person or thing, and it is formed in relation to the past, present and future conditions of its object; the right horoscope tells you therefore about the conditions of a person.

All mystery is hidden in a name. The knowledge of everything rests on first knowing its name, and knowledge is not complete which is devoid of name. Mastery depends upon knowledge. Man cannot master a thing of which he has no knowledge. All blessings and benefits derived from earth or heaven are gained by mastery which depends upon knowledge, knowledge depending upon name. Man without the knowledge of the name of a thing is ignorant, and the ignorant are powerless, for man has no hold over any thing of which he has no knowledge.

The reason of man's greatness is the scope of knowledge with which he is gifted, all the mystery of which lies in his recognition of the difference between things and beings. This gives man superiority not only over all the creatures of earth, but it even makes him excel the Angels, the hosts of heaven. The Koran explains it in the following words "We are going to place a substitute on earth" they said, "Wilt Thou place there one who will do evil therein and shed blood, while we celebrate Thy praise and sanctify Thee?" God answered, "Verily We know that which ye know not," and He taught Adam the names of all things, and then proposed them to the Angels, and said, "Declare unto me the names of these things if ye say truth." They answered, "Praise be unto Thee, we have no knowledge, but what Thou teachest us, for Thou art all-knowing and wise." God said, "O! Adam, tell them their names." And when Adam came he told their names. See also Genesis ii. 19.

Every name reveals to the Seer the past, present, and the future of that which it covers.

Name is not only significant of form but of character as well. The meaning of name plays an important part in man's life, and the sound, the vowels in the name, the rhythm, number, and nature of the letters which compose it, the mystical numbers, symbol, and planet, as well as the root from which it is derived, and the effect which it produces, all disclose their secret to the Seer.

The meaning of a name has a great influence upon its possessor as well as upon others.

From the sound of the letters and the word they compose the mystic understand much about the character and fate of a person. An intelligent person generally gets the idea from the sound of letters that compose a name whether it is beautiful or ugly, soft or hard, consonant or dissonant but does not know what makes it so; the one who understands knows why it is so.

Letters singly or together are either pronounced smoothly or with difficulty and have their effect accordingly upon oneself and upon another. Names that are smooth and soft sounding make a soft effect upon the speaker and listener whereas hard sounding names have a contrary effect. Man naturally calls soft things by smooth names and hard things by hard-sounding names as for instance flower and rock, wool and flint, etc. Language, and especially name shows the class of people and character of families, communities and races. Vowels play a great part in the name and its

influence. "E" and "I" denote Jemal the
feminine quality of grace, wisdom, beauty and
receptivity, "O" and "U" denote Jelal, the
masculine quality of power and expression.
"A" denotes Kemal which is significant of the
perfection in which both these qualities are
centered.

The above-named vowels in the
composition of the name have an effect
beginning, centre or end.

Fate in Sanskrit is called Karma, meaning
the rhythm of past actions. The influence of
rhythm suggested by a name has an effect
upon the entity whose name it is as well as
upon those who call him by that name.
Evenness of rhythm gives balance while
unevenness causes a lack of balance. The
beauty of rhythm beautifies the character of
man.

By rhythm is meant the way in which the
name begins and how it ends, whether evenly
or unevenly, on the accent or before the accent.
The accent falling on the beginning, middle
or end varies the effect which plays a part in
a person's character and fate. The rhythm of
the name suggests the main thing in life,
balance or its lack. Lack of balance is a
deficiency in character and causes adversity
in life. The number of letters plays a great
part in the name of a person. An even number
shows beauty and wisdom, and an odd number
shows love and power.

Number plays a great part in life and especially in name. Each letter in the constitution of a name has its numeric value, in Oriental science it is called Jafar. By this system not only names are given to buildings, objects and people conveying their period of commencement and finishing, but the combination of these numbers conveys to the Seer its mystical effect.

Names have a psychic effect upon their owners and even upon surroundings. The names of elementals and Djins, the sacred Names of God, and the holy names of the Prophets and Saints written according to the law of their numeric value act as a magical charm for the accomplishment of different objects in life, and by the combination of such written or repeated in their numeric form wonders are performed.

Every letter either singly or when grouped in a word produces a picture which tells its secret to the Seer.

For instance X makes a cross and O zero, both of which have a meaning. The alphabet used in modern times is a corruption of the original ones; the old Arabic and Persian writings which are found on the arches, walls, hems of garments, on brass vessels and carpets are of most perfect and beautiful design. A great symbolic significance may be seen in the Chinese, Japanese, Sanskrit and other ancient alphabets. Every line, dot and curve has a meaning. The ancients used to write every name not with different letters but as a picture signifying what they wished to express; the picture was divided into different parts and each part was used to represent a certain sound and in this way the alphabets were made. By this break the true picture is lost, but a certain likeness may still be traced. Even in the present day although we have a most corrupted form of writing, still from the appearance of a certain name, in whatever language it may be written a person's life, fate or character may be read. For instance, a name beginning with I shows a steadfast and righteous ego, uniqueness and love of God and the pursuit of truth. E shows a shy and backward nature and an interest in three directions. As one letter makes a picture in the same way a whole come from man, and one can read from the form of the hand the word Allah written. The Christian name has a greater influence than the surname. Sometimes a nickname has a still greater effect. The effect of the name is according to its use, the more it is used the greater the effect. Shortened names such as May for Mary, or Bill or Willie for William, lessen the effect of the name to part. The names given by the Holy Ones have a double effect, that of the name itself and that of the will of the holy One Who has given it. Moula Box, the greatest musician in India of his day, was given this name by a Fakir who was charmed on hearing his music, and it means "God bless." After taking this name he had success wherever he went, and was blessed with merit and reward, both of which are the rare gifts of God.

There are many instances to be found where a change of name has brought an entire change in man's life. We read in the Bible that the blessing of Jacob was the name Israel given to him by the Angel.

In the Koran, Mohammed is constantly addressed by a special name having its effect not only on the life of the prophet, but on his followers who adopted and worked psychically with any of these names. Sufis have for ages experienced the mystical value of these names. Among Sufis the Murshid gives to his pupils the name "Talib," or "Mureed" which is to give him in time the identity of the name.

V

Form

The light from which all life comes exists in three aspects, namely the aspect which manifests as intelligence; the light of the abstract and the light of the sun. The activity of this one light functions in three different aspects. The first aspect is caused by a slow and solemn activity in the Eternal Consciousness which may be called consciousness or intelligence. It is intelligence when there in nothing before it to be conscious of, and when there is something intelligible before it, the same intelligence becomes consciousness. A normal activity in the light of intelligence cause the light of the abstract at the time when the abstract sound turns into light. This light becomes a torch for the Seer who is journeying towards the eternal goal. The same light in its intense activity appears as the sun. No person would readily believe that the intelligence, abstract light, and the sun are one and the same, yet language cannot contradict itself, and all three have always been called by the name of light.

These three aspects of the One Light are the idea that lies behind the doctrine of the Trinity, and that of "Trimurti" that existed thousands of years before Christianity among the Hindus; and which denotes the One, the One being three. Substance commences to develop from radium to an atom, but before this it exists as a vibration. What man sees, he accepts as something existent and what he cannot see, does not exist for him. All that man perceives, sees and feels is matter, and that which is the source and cause of all is spirit.

The philosophy of form may be understood by the study of the process through which the life unseen manifests into the seen. As the fine waves produce light. This is the manner in which the unseen, incomprehensible, and imperceptible life becomes gradually known, by first becoming audible and then visible, and this is the origin and only source of all form.

The sun therefore is the first form seen by the eyes, and is the origin and source of all forms in the objective world, and as such it has been worshipped by the ancients as God, and we can trace the origin of all religions in that mother-religion. We may trace this philosophy in the words of Shamstabriz: "When the Sun showed his face then appeared the faces and forms of all worlds. His Beauty showed their beauty; in His brightness they shone out; so by His rays we saw and knew and named them."

All the myriad colors in the universe are but the different grades and shades of light, the creator of all elements, which has decorated the heavens so beautifully with sun, moon, planets, and stars; which has made the land and water, with all the beauties of the lower spheres, in some parts dull and in some parts bright, which man has named light and shade. The sun, moon, planets and stars, the brilliance of electricity, the lesser light of gas, lamp, candle, coal and wood, all show the sun re-appearing in different forms; the sun is reflected in all things, be they dull pebbles or sparkling diamonds, and their radiance is according to their capability of reflection. This shows that light is the one and only source, and is the cause of the whole creation. "God is the light of the heaven and of the earth." Koran. "And God said: Let there be light, and there was Light." Genesis I. 3.

All forms in whatever plane they exist, are moulded under the law of affinity. Every atom attracts towards itself the atom of its own element; every positive atom attracts the negative atom of its own element and the negative attracts the positive; yet each attraction is different and distinct; these atoms group together and make a form. The atoms of the abstract plane group together and make forms of light and color, these and all different forms of the mental plane are composed of the atoms of that plane, these are seen by the mind's eye and are called imagination. In the physical plane this process may be seen in a more concrete form.

The mystic sees in the abstract plane one or another element predominating at a certain time, either ether, air fire, water or earth. Every element in the finer forces of life is rendered intelligible by the direction of its activity and color, and the various forms of light show its different rates of activity; as for instance the feeling of humor develops into greater humor, and sadness into a deeper sorrow, so it is with the imagination, every pleasant thought develops pleasure and expands into a still pleasanter thought, and every disagreeable imagination grows and becomes more intense. Again on the physical plane we not only see men dwelling together in cities and villages, but even beasts and birds living in flocks and herds; coal is found in the coal mine, and gold in the gold mine; the forest contains thousands of trees, whereas the desert holds not a single one. All this proves the power of affinity which collects and groups the atoms of like kind, and makes of them numerous forms, thereby creating an illusion before the eye of man who forgets the One Source in the manifestation of variety.

The direction taken by every element to make a form depends upon the nature of its activity. For instance, an activity following a straight direction, shows the earth element, a downward direction, the water element, in an upward direction, the fire element, the activity that moves in a zig-zag direction shows the air element, and the form taken by ether is indistinct and misty. Therefore the nature of all things is made plain to the Seer by their form and shape, and from their color their element is known, yellow being the color of earth, green of water, red of fire, blue of air, and grey of ether. The mingling of these elements produces mixed colors which vary into innumerable shades and tones, and the variety of color in nature bears evidence to the unlimited life behind it.

Every activity of vibrations produces a certain sound, according to its dome of resonance, and according to the capacity of the mould the form is shaped.

This proves the idea of the ancient Hindu word Nada Brahma, which means sound, the Creator God.

By the law of construction and destruction as well as by addition and reduction the different forms in this objective world group together and change. A close study of the constant grouping and dispersing of the clouds will reveal many different forms within the process which can be seen all through nature. The construction and destruction, addition and reduction in forms all take place under the influence of time and space. Each form is shaped and changed subject to this law, for the substance differs according to the length, breadth, depth, height, figure and shape of the mould where the form is modelled, and the features are formed according to the impression pressed upon it. It takes time to make a young and tender leaf green, and again to change it from green to red and yellow; and it is space that makes of water either a ditch, well, pond, stream, river or the ocean.

The dissimilarity in the features of various races in different periods can be accounted for by the law of time and space, together with climatic and racial causes. The Afghans resemble the natives of the Punjab, and the Singalese the people of Madras; Arabs are similar in feature to the Japanese, Tibetans resemble the natives of Bhutan, and the Burmese closely resemble the Siamese. All this proves that the proximity of the land which they inhabit is largely the cause of likeness in feature. As wide as is the distance of space, so wide is the difference in feature among people. The similarity in form of germs, worms, and insects is accounted for by the same reason. Twin children as a rule resemble each other more closely than other children.

Form depends mostly upon reflection; it is the reflection of the sun in the moon that makes the moon appear round like the sun. All the lower creation evolves by the same law. Animals which begin to resemble man are among those which are in his surroundings, and see him daily. A man who has the care of animals begins to resemble them, and we see that the butler of a colonel has the bearing of a soldier, and a maid working in a nunnery in time becomes like a nun.

As all things are subject to change, no one thing is the same as it was a moment before, although change from bud to blossom and in fruit from the unripe to the ripe state.

Even stones change, and some among them have been known to become perceptibly altered even in the course of twenty-four hours.

Time has great influence upon all things and beings as may be seen by the change from infancy to youth, and from middle age to old age. In Sanskrit therefore time is called Kal which means destruction, as no change is possible without destruction; in other words destruction may be described as change. All things natural and artificial that we see today differ vastly in their form from what they were several thousand years ago, and not only can this be noticed in such things as fruit, flowers, birds and animals, but also in the human race; for from time to time the structure of man has undergone various changes.

The form of man is divided into two parts, each part having its special attributes. The head is the spiritual body, and the lower part the material body. Therefore, in comparison with the body, the head has far greater importance; thereby one individual is able to recognize another, as the head is the only distinctive part of man. The face is expressive of man's nature and condition in life, also of his past, present and future.

When asked if the face would be burned in the fire of hell, the Prophet made answer, "No, the face will not be burned, for Allah hath said, We have modelled man on Our Own Image."

The likeness between things and beings, as well as between beasts and birds, animals and man can tell us a great deal about the secret of their nature. The sciences of Phrenology and Physiology were discovered not only by examining the lives of men of various features, but chiefly by studying the similarity that exists between them and animals. For instance a man having the features of a tiger will have a dominant nature, coupled with courage anger and cruelty. A man with a face resembling a horse, is by nature subservient; a man with a face like a dog will have a pugnacious tendency while a mouse-like face shows timidity.

There are four sources from which the human face and form are derived, and these account for the changes which take place in them; these are, the inherent attributes of his soul; the influence of his heritage; the impressions of his surroundings and lastly the impression of himself, and of his thoughts and deeds, the clothes he wears, the food he eats, the air he breathes, and the way he lives. In the first of these sources man is helpless for he has no choice; it was not the desire of the tiger to be a tiger, neither did a monkey choose to be a monkey, and it was not the choice of the infant to be born a male or a female. This proves that the first source of man's form depends upon the inherent attributes brought by his soul. Words never can express adequately the wisdom of the creator who not only fashioned and formed the world, but to each being has given the form suited to his needs; the animals of the cold zones are provided with thick fur as a protection against the cold; to the beasts of the tropics a suitable form is given; the birds of the sea have wings fit for the sea, and those of the earth are provided with wings suitable for the earth. Birds and animals have forms which accord with their habits in life. The form of man proclaims his grade of evolution, his nature, his past and present, as well as his race, nation and surroundings, character and fate.

In the second instance man inherits beauty or its opposite from his ancestors, but in the third his form depends upon how he builds it. The build of his form depends upon the balance and regularity of his life, and upon the impressions he receives from the world, for in accordance with the attitude he takes towards life his every thought and action adds or takes away, or removes to another place the atoms of his body, thus forming the lines and muscles of form and feature. For instance, the face of man speaks his joy, sorrow, pleasure, displeasure, sincerity, insincerity, and all that is developed in him. The muscles of his head tell the phrenologist his condition in life. There is a form in the thought and feelings which produce a beautiful or ugly effect. It is the nature of evolution for all beings from the lowest to the highest stage of manifestation to evolve by being connected with a more perfect form. Animals approaching man in their evolution resemble primitive man, and animals in contact with man acquire in their form traces of the likeness of man. This may be understood by a close study of the features of man in the past, and of the improvement which has been made in them. The nature of creation is that it is progressing always towards beauty. "God is beautiful, and He loves beauty" (Koran). The nature of the body is to beautify itself; the nature of the mind is to have beautiful thoughts; the longing of the heart is for beautiful feelings. Therefore an infant should grow more beautiful every day, and ignorance seeks to become intelligence. When the progress is in a contrary direction, it shows that the individual has lost the track of natural progress. There are two forms, the natural and the artificial, the latter being a copy of the former.

VI

Rhythm

Motion is the significance of life, and the law of motion is rhythm. Rhythm is life disguised in motion and in its every guise it seems to attract the attention of man, from a child who is pleased with the moving of a rattle and is soothed by the swing of its cradle, to a grown person whose every game, sport, and enjoyment has rhythm disguised in it in some way or another, whether it is a game of tennis, cricket or golf, as well as boxing and wrestling. Again in the intellectual amusements of man, both poetry and music, vocal or instrumental, have rhythm as their very spirit and life. There is a saying in Sanskrit that tone is the mother of nature but that rhythm is its father. An infant once given the habit of a regular time for his food, demands it at that time, although he has no idea of time. This is accounted for by the fact that the very nature of life is rhythm. The infant begins its life on earth by moving its arms and legs, thus showing the rhythm of its nature, and illustrating the philosophy which teaches that rhythm is the sign of life. The inclination to dance shown by every man illustrates also that innate nature of beauty which chooses rhythm for its expression.

Rhythm produces an ecstasy which is inexplicable, and incomparable with any other source of intoxication. This is why the dance has been the most fascinating pastime of all people, both civilized and savage, and has delighted alike Saint and sinner. The races which show a tendency for strongly accentuated rhythm must be vigorous by nature. Rag-time, which is so popular in these days, has come from the Negroes, and the syncopation is the secret of its charm and is the natural expression of their racial rhythm.

The rhythm of rag-time arouses a kind of life among performers and audience alike, and it is the love of this life that has given such popularity to the jazz band. The dances among many wild tribes in different parts of the world show a most pronounced rhythm, which proves that rhythm is not a culture, but is natural. Amongst Europeans, the Spanish, Poles, Hungarians and Russians show the greatest tendency toward rhythm.

The secret of the success of the Russian Ballet and the Spanish Dance lies in their exquisite rhythm. Among the Asiatic races the music of the Mongolians is chiefly based on rhythm, it being more pronounced than

melody in their music. In Turkish and Persian
Music rhythm is also pronounced, and among
the Arabs the variety of rhythms is vast. In
India, however, the culture of rhythm has
reached perfection, an expert musician in
India improvises a melody, keeping the same
time throughout the whole improvisation. In
order to become a master musician in India,
one must master thoroughly not only *raga*, the
scale, but also *tal*, the rhythm. Indians as a
race are naturally inclined to rhythm; their
dance *Tandava Nritya*, the dance of the South,
is an expression of rhythm through movement.

In the Hindu science of music there are
five different rhythms which are generally
derived from the study of nature:

1. **Chatura,** the rhythm of four beats, which
was invented by Devas or Divine men.

2. **Tisra,** the rhythm of three beats,
invented by Rishis, the Saints.

3. **Khanda,** the rhythm of five beats,
invented by the Rakshasas.

4. **Misra,** the rhythm of seven beats,
invented by the people.

5. **Sankrian,** the rhythm of nine beats, in
vented by the commercial class.

Mahadeva, the great Lord of the Yogis was
the dancer of Tandava Nritya and his Consort
Parvati danced the Lassia Nritya.

The traditions of the Hindus have as a
most sacred record the mystical legend of their
Lord Shri Krishna as dancing with the Gopis.

The story relates how Krishna, the charming youthful Lord of the Hindus, was moving among the dwellings of the cowherds and every maiden attracted by his beauty and charm asked him to dance with her; he promised every maiden that asked him that he would dance with her on the night of the full moon. On the night of the full moon there assembled sixteen hundred Gopis, and the miracle of Krishna was performed when he appeared as a separate Krishna to each Gopi, and all of them danced with their beloved Lord at one and the same time. There is a tradition in Islam, where music, dancing and all amusements and light occupations are strictly prohibited, that on one occasion it being a holiday, the Prophet called His wife Ayesha to look at the dance and listen to the music of some street musicians. In the meantime his great Khalif happened to come by and was shocked at seeing the Prophet who had prohibited such things himself permitting music in front of his house. When he stopped the music of the street players pointing out to them that it was the house of the Prophet, Mohammed requested that they might continue, saying that it was a holiday, and "There in no heart that does not move with the motion or rhythm."

In the traditions of the Sufis Rakhs, the Sacred Dance of spiritual ecstasy which even now is prevalent among the Sufis of the East, is traced from the time when contemplation upon the Creator impressed the wonderful reality of his vision so deeply on the heart of Jellad-ud-in Rumi, that he became entirely absorbed in the whole and single immanence of nature, and took a rhythmic turn which caused the skirt of his garment to form a circle, and the movements of his hands and neck made a circle, and it is the memory of this moment of vision that is celebrated in the dance of Dervishes. Even in the lower creation among beasts and birds, their joy is always expressed in dance; a bird like the peacock, when conscious of his beauty and of the beauty of the forest around him, expresses his joy in dance. Dance arouses passion and emotion in all living creatures.

In the East, and especially in India, where the life of people for centuries has been based on psychological principles, in the Royal Processions or at Durbars the beating of the drums is taken as the means of making an impression of kingly grandeur upon the minds of people; and the same beating of drums takes place at wedding ceremonies and at the services in the Temples.

Sufis, in order to awaken that emotional nature which is generally asleep in man, have a rhythmic practice which sets the whole mechanism of body and mind to rhythm. There exists in all people, either consciously or unconsciously, a tendency toward rhythm. Among European nations the expression of pleasure is shown by the clapping of the hands; a farewell sign is made by the waving of the hand which makes rhythm.

All labor and toil, however hard and difficult, is made easy by the power of rhythm in some way or another, this idea opens to the thinker a still deeper scope for the study of life.

Rhythm in its every guise, be it called game, play, amusement, poetry, music or dance is the very nature of man's whole constitution. When the entire mechanism of his body is working in a rhythm, the beat of the pulse, of the heart, of the head, the circulation of the blood, hunger and thirst, all show rhythm, and it is the breaking of rhythm that is called disease. When the child is crying and the mother does not know what ails him, she holds him in her arms on his chest and pats him on the back. This sets the circulation of the blood, the pulsations and the whole mechanism of the body to rhythm; in other words sets the body in order, and soothes the child. The nursery rhyme "Pat-a-cake," which is known all the world over in some form or another, cures a child of fretfulness by setting his whole being to rhythm.

Therefore physicians depend more upon the examination of the pulse than on anything else in discovering the true nature of disease, together with the examination of the beat of the heart and the movement of the lungs in the chest and back.

Rhythm plays a most important part not only in the body, but in the mind also; the change form joy to sorrow, the rising and fall of thoughts, and the whole working of the mind show rhythm, and all confusion and despair seem to be accounted for by the lack of rhythm in mind.

In the ancient times healers in the East, and especially those in India, when healing a patient of any complaint of a psychological character, known either as an obsession or an effect of magic, excited the emotional nature of the patient by the emphatic rhythm of their drum and song, at the same time making the patient swing his head up and down to the time of the music. This aroused his emotions and prompted him to tell the secret of his complaint which hitherto had been hidden under the cover of fear, convention, and forms of society. The patient confessed everything to the healer under the spell produced by the rhythm, and the healer was enabled to discover the source of the malady.

The words thoughtful and thoughtless signify a rhythmic or unrhythmic state of the mind, and balance which is the only upholding power in life which is kept by rhythm. Respiration which keeps mind and body connected and which links the mind and soul, consists in keeping rhythm every moment when awake or asleep; inhaling and exhaling may be likened to the moving and swinging of the pendulum of a clock. As all strength and energy is maintained by breath, and as breath is the sign of life, and its nature is to flow alternately on the right and left side, all this proves rhythm to be life's greatest significance. As rhythm is innate in man and maintains his health, so upon rhythm depend all man's affairs in life, his success, his failure, his right acts and his wrong acts, all are accounted for some way or the other by the change of rhythm. The instinct of flying in the bird is a rhythmic movement of the wings; and it is the some tendency of rhythmic contraction which makes the fish to swim and the snake to glide. A keen observation shows that the whole universe is a single mechanism working by the law of rhythm; the rise and fall of the waves, the ebb and flow of the tide, the waxing and waning of the moon, the sunrise and the sunset, the change of the seasons, the moving of the earth and of the planets, the whole cosmic system and the constitution of the entire universe are working under the law of rhythm. Cycles of rhythm with major cycles and minor cycles interpenetrating uphold the whole creation in their swing. This demonstrates the origin of manifestation; that motion has sprung from the still life, and every motion as a necessity must result in a dual aspect. As soon as you move a stick, the single movement will make two points, the one where it starts and the other where it ends, the one strong and the other weak, to which a music conductor will count "one, two"; "one, two," a strong accent and a weak accent; one motion with two effects, each distinct and different from the other. It is this mystery that lies hidden under the dual aspects in all phases and forms of life and the reason, cause, and significance of all life is found in rhythm. There is a psychological conception about rhythms used in poetry or music which may be explained thus, that every rhythm has a certain effect, not only upon the physical and mental bodies of the poet, or on him for whom the poetry is written; upon the musician or on him to whom the song is sung, but even upon their life's affairs; that is to say the belief is that it can bring good or bad luck to the poet and musician or to the one who listens. The idea is that rhythm is hidden under the root of every activity, constructive or destructive, so that on the rhythm of every activity the fate of the affair depends. Expressions used in everyday speech such as, "He was too late," or, " it was done too soon," or "That was done in time," all show the influence of rhythm upon the affair. Instances such as the sinking of the Titanic, and the amazing changes that took place during the late war, if keenly studied can be accounted for by rhythm working in both mental and physical spheres.

There is a superstition among Indians that when somebody present yawns, some one else who is present must either snap his fingers or clap his hands. The hidden meaning of this is that a yawn is significant of the slowing down of the rhythm, and that by clicking the fingers or clapping the hands one is supposed to bring the rhythm up to its original state. A Moslem child when reading the Koran moves his head backwards and forwards; this is popularly supposed to be a respectful bow to the sacred words that he reads but psychologically speaking it helps him to memorize the Koran by regulating the circulation, making the brain a receptive vehicle, as when filling a bottle one sometimes must shake it in order to make more room. This also may be seen when a person nods the head in accepting an idea or shakes it when he cannot take it in. The mechanism of every kind of machinery that works by itself is arranged and kept going by the law of rhythm, and this is another proof of the fact that the whole mechanism of the universe is based on the law of rhythm.

VII

Music

When we pay attention to nature's music, we find that every thing on the earth contributes to its harmony. The trees joyously wave their branches to the rhythm of the wind; the sound of the sea, the murmuring of the breeze, the whistling of the wind through rocks, hills, and mountains; the flash of the lightning, and the crash of the thunder; the harmony of the sun and moon, the movements of the stars and planets, the blooming of the flower, the fading of the leaf, the regular alternation of morning, evening, noon, and night, all reveal to the Seer the music of nature.

The insects have their concerts and ballets, and the choirs of birds chant in unison their hymns of praise. Dogs and cats have their orgies, foxes and wolves have their *soirees-musicales* in the forest, while tigers and lions hold their operas in the wilderness, Music is the only means of understanding among birds and beasts. This may be seen by the gradation of their pitch and the volume of their tone, the manner of their tune, the number of repetitions and the duration of their various sounds, which convey to their fellow creatures the time for joining the flock, the warning of coming danger, the declaration of war, the feeling of love, and the sense of sympathy, displeasure, passion, anger, fear and jealousy; making a language of itself.

In man breath is a constant tone, and the beat of the heart, pulse, and head keeps the rhythm continually. An infant responds to music before he has learnt how to speak; he moves his hands and feet in time, and expresses his pleasure and pain in different tones.

In the beginning of human creation, no language such as we now have, existed, but only music. Man first expressed his thoughts and feelings by low and high, slow and prolonged sounds. The depth of his tone showed his strength and power; and the height of his pitch expressed love and wisdom. Man conveyed his sincerity, insincerity, inclination, disinclination, pleasure or displeasure, by the variety of his musical expressions.

The tongue touching various points in the mouth and the opening and the closing of the lips in different ways, produced the variety of sounds. The grouping of the sounds made words conveying different meanings in their various modes of expression. This gradually transformed music into a language but language could never free itself from music.

A word spoken in a certain tone shows subservience, and the same word spoken in a different tone expresses command; a word spoken in a certain pitch shows kindness, and the same word spoken in a different pitch expresses coldness. Words spoken in certain rhythm show willingness, and the same words express unwillingness when spoken at a different degree of speed. Up to the present day the ancient languages Sanskrit, Arabic and Hebrew cannot be mastered by simply learning the words, pronunciation and grammar, because a particular rhythmic and tonal expression is needed. The word in itself is frequently insufficient to express the meaning clearly. The student of language by keen study can discover this. Even modern languages are but a simplification of music. No words of any language can be spoken in one and the same way without the distinction of tone, pitch, rhythm, accent, pause and rest. A language however simple cannot exist without music in it, music gives it a concrete expression. It is therefore that a foreign language is rarely perfectly spoken; the words are learnt, but the music is not mastered.

Language may be called the simplification of music; music is hidden within it as the soul is hidden in the body; at each step toward simplification the language has lost some of its music. A study of ancient traditions reveals that the first Divine Messages were given in song; as were the Psalms of David, The Song of Solomon, the Gathas of Zoroaster, and the Gita of Krishna.

When language became more complex it closed as it were one wing, the sense of tone; keeping the other wing, the sense of rhythm, outspread. This made poetry, a subject distinct and separate from music. In ancient times religions, philosophies, sciences and arts were expressed in poetry. The Vedas, Puranas, Ramayana, Mahabaharata, Zend Avesta, Kabala, and Bible are to be found in verse, as well as different arts and sciences in the ancient languages. Among the scriptures the only work in prose is the Koran, and even this is not devoid of poetry. In the East, even in recent times, not only manuscripts of science, art, and literature were written in poetry, but the learned even discoursed in verse. In the next stage, man freed the language from the bond of rhythm and made prose out of poetry. Although man has tried to free language from the trammels of tone and rhythm, the spirit of music still exists. Man prefers to hear poetry recited and prose well read, which is in itself a proof of the soul seeking music even in the spoken word.

The crooning song of the mother soothes the infant and makes him sleep, and lively music gives him an inclination to dance. It is music which doubles the courage and strength of a soldier when marching toward the field of battle. In the East, when the caravans travel form place to place on a pilgrimage, they sing as they go. In India the coolies sing when at work, and the rhythm of the music makes the hardest labor become easy for them.

The ancient legend tells how the angels sang at the command of God to induce the unwilling soul to enter the body of Adam. The soul, intoxicated by the song of the angels, entered the body which it regarded as a prison. All spiritualists who have really sounded the depths of spiritualism have realized that there is no better means of attracting the spirits from their plane of freedom to the outer plane than by music. They make use of different instruments that appeal to a certain spirit, and sing songs that have a special effect upon the particular spirit with whom they wish to communicate. There is no magic like music to make an effect upon the human soul.

The taste for music is an inborn instinct in man, and it first shows in the infant.

Music is known to a child from his cradle, but as he grows in this world of delusion, his mind becomes absorbed in so many and varied objects that he loses the aptitude for music which his soul possessed. When grown-up he enjoys and appreciates music in accordance with his grade of evolution, and with the state of the surroundings in which he has been born and brought up; the man of the wilderness sings his wild lays, and the man of the city his popular song. The more refined man becomes, the finer music he enjoys. The influence of character in every man creates a tendency for music akin to it; in other words the gay man enjoys light music, while the serious minded person prefers classical; the intellectual man takes delight in technique, while the simpleton is satisfied with his drum.

There are five different aspects of the art of music: 1. The popular, that which induces motion of the body; 2. Technical, that which satisfies the intellect; 3. Artistic, that which has beauty and grace; 4. Appealing, that which pierces the heart; 5. Uplifting, in which the soul hears the music of the spheres.

The effect of music depends, not only on the proficiency, but also upon the evolution of the performer. Its effect upon the listener is in accordance with his knowledge and evolution, for this reason the value of music differs with each individual. For a self-satisfied person there is no chance of progress, because he clings contentedly to his taste according to his state of evolution, refusing to advance a step higher than his present level. He who gradually progresses along the path of music, in the end attains to the highest perfection. No other art can inspire and sweeten the personality like music; the lover of music attains sooner or later to the most sublime field of thought.

India has preserved the mysticism of tone and pitch discovered by the ancients, and this their music itself signifies.

Indian music is based upon the principle of the *Raga* which shows it to be akin to nature. It has avoided the limitations of technique by adopting a purely inspirational method.

Ragas are derived from five different sources. 1. The mathematical law of variety. 2. The inspiration of the mystics. 3. The imagination of the musicians. 4. The natural lays peculiar to the people residing in different parts of the land. 5. The idealization of the poets who made a world of *ragas*, calling one *rag*, the male, another *ragini*, the female, and others *putra*, sons; and *bharja*, daughters in law.

Raga is called the male theme because of its creative and positive nature; *Ragini* is termed the female theme on account of its responsive and fine quality. *Putras* are such themes as are derived from the comingling of *ragas* and *raginis*, in them can be found a likeness to the raga and the *ragini* from which they are derived. *Bharja* is the corresponding theme which responds to the *putra*. There are six ragas, thirty-six *raginis*, six belonging to each raga, forty-eight *putras*, and forty-eight *bharjas*, which constitute this family.

Each *raga* has an administration of its own including a chief, Mukhya, the key note; a

king, Wadi, a principal note; Sumwadi, a
minister, a subordinate note; Anuwadi, an
enemy, a dissonant note. This gives to the
student of the *raga* a clear conception of its
use. Each *raga* has its image distinct from the
other. This shows the highest reach of
imagination.

The poets have pictured the images of
ragas, as each aspect of life its picture clear
in the imagination of the intelligent. The
ancient Gods and Goddesses were simply
pictures of the different aspects of life, and in
order to teach the worship of the immanence
of God in nature these various pictures were
placed in the temples, that God in His every
aspect of manifestation might be worshipped.
The same idea has been worked out in the
images of ragas, which form in a delicate
imagination the type, form, figure, action,
expression and effect of the idea.

Every hour of the day night, every day,
week, month and season has its influence
upon man's physical and mental condition. In
the same way each raga has power upon the
sphere, as well as upon the health and mind
of man; the same effect as that which the
different times show in life subject to the
cosmic law. By the knowledge of both time and
raga the wise have connected them to suit each
other. There are instances in ancient tradition
when birds and animals were charmed by the
flute of Krishna, rocks were melted by the song

of Orpheus, and the *Deepak Raga* sung by
Tansen lighted all the torches; while he
himself was burnt by reason of the inner fire
his song produced. Even today the snakes are
charmed by the *Pungi* of the snake charmers
in India. All this shows us how the ancients
must have dived into the most mysterious
ocean of music.

The secret of composition lies in sustaining
the tone as solidly and as long as possible
through all its different degrees; a break
destroys its life, grace, power and magnetism,
just as the breath holds life, and has all grace,
power and magnetism. There are some notes
that need a longer life than others, according
to their character and purpose.

In a true composition a miniature of
nature's music is seen. The effects of thunder,
rain, and storm, and the pictures of hills and
rivers make music a real art. Although art is
an improvisation on nature, yet it is only
genuine when it keeps close to nature. The
music which expresses the nature and
character of individuals, nations or races is
still higher. The highest and most ideal form
of composition is that which expresses life,
character, emotions and feelings, for this is
the inner world which is only seen by the eye
of mind. A genius uses music as a language to
express fully without the help of words
whatever he may wish to be known, for music,

a perfect and universal language, can express feeling more comprehensively than any tongue.

Music loses its freedom by being subject to the laws of technique, but Mystics in their sacred music, regardless of the world's praise, free both their composition and improvisations from the limitations of technicality.

The art of music in the East is called Kala, and has three aspects, vocal, instrumental, and motional.

Vocal music is considered to be the highest, for it is natural; the effect produced by an instrument, which is merely a machine, cannot be compared with that of the human voice. However perfect strings may be, they cannot make the same impression on the listener as the voice which comes direct from the soul as breath, and has been brought to the surface through the medium of the mind and vocal organs of the body. When the soul desires to express itself in voice, it first causes an activity in the mind, and the mind by mental plane, which in due course develops and runs as breath through the regions of the abdomen, lungs, mouth, throat, and nasal organs, vibrating the air all through, until they manifest on the surface as voice. The voice therefore naturally expresses the attitude of mind whether true or false, sincere or insincere.

The voice has all the magnetism which an instrument lacks for voice is nature's ideal instrument, upon which all other instruments of the world are modelled.

The effect produced by singing depends upon the depth of feeling of the singer. The voice of a sympathetic singer is quite different from that of one who is heartless. However artificially cultivated a voice may be, it will never produce feeling, grace and beauty unless the heart be cultivated also. Singing has a twofold source of interest, the grace of music and the beauty of poetry. In proportion as the singer feels the words he sings, an effect is produced upon the listeners; his heart, so to speak, accompanies the song.

Although the sound produced by an instrument cannot be produced by the voice, yet the instrument is absolutely dependent upon man. This explains clearly how the soul makes use of the mind, and how the mind rules the body yet the body seems to work, not the mind, and the soul is left out of the question. When man hears the sound of the instrument and sees the hand of the player at work, he does not see the mind working behind and the phenomenon of the soul.

At each step from the inner being to the surface there is an apparent improvement, which appears to be more positive, yet every step towards the surface entails limitation and dependence.

There is sound, although tone manifests more clearly through a sonorous body than through a solid one, the former being open to vibrations while the latter is closed. All things which give a clear sound show life, while solid bodies choked up with substance seem dead. Resonance is the reserving of tone, in other words it is the rebound of tone which produces an echo. On this principle all instruments are made, the difference lying in the quality and quantity of the tone, which depend upon the construction of the instrument. The instruments of percussion such as the *Tabla*, or the drum, are suited for practical music, and stringed instruments like the *Sitar*, violin or harp are meant for artistic music. The *vina* is especially constructed to concentrate the vibrations; as it gives a faint sound, audible to the player only, it is used in meditation. The effect of instrumental music also depends upon the evolution of man who expresses with the tips of his fingers upon the instrument his grade of evolution; in other words his soul speaks through the instrument. Man's state of mind can be read by his touch upon any instrument, for however great an expert he may be, he cannot produce by mere skill without a developed feeling within himself the grace and beauty which appeals to the heart.

Wind instruments like the flute and the Algosa, especially express the heart quality for they are played with the breath which is the very life therefore they kindle the heart's fire.

Instruments stringed with gut have a living effect, for they come from a living creature which once had a heart; those stringed with wire have a thrilling effect and the instruments of percussion such as the drum have a stimulating and animating effect upon man.

After vocal and instrumental music comes the motional music of dance. Motion is the nature of vibration. Every motion contains within itself a thought and feeling. This art is innate in man; an infant's first pleasure in life is to amuse himself with the movement of hands and feet, a child on hearing music begins to move. Even beasts and birds express their joy in motion. The peacock proud in the vision of his beauty displays his vanity in dance, likewise the cobra unfolds his hood and rocks his body on hearing the music of the Pungi. All this proves that motion is the sign of life and when accompanied with music it sets both the performer and onlooker in motion.

The Mystics have always looked upon this subject as a sacred art. In the Hebrew scriptures we find David dancing before the Lord, and the Gods and Goddesses of the Greeks, Egyptians, Buddhists, and Brahmans are represented in different poses, all having a certain meaning and philosophy, relating to the great Cosmic Dance which is evolution.

Even up to the present time among Sufis in the East dancing takes place at their sacred meetings called Suma, for dancing is the outcome of joy; the dervishes at the Suma give an outlet to their ecstasy in Rakhs which is regarded with great respect and reverence by those present, and is in itself a sacred ceremony.

The art of dancing has greatly degenerated owing to its misuse. People for the most part dance either for the sake of amusement or exercise, often abusing the art in their frivolity.

Tune and rhythm have a tendency to produce an inclination for dance. To sum up, dancing may be said to be a graceful expression of thought and feeling without uttering a word. It may be used also to impress the soul by movement, by producing an ideal picture before it. When beauty of movement is taken as the presentment of the Divine Ideal, then the dance becomes sacred.

The music of life shows its melody and harmony is our daily experiences. Every spoken word is either a time or a false note, according to the scale of our ideal. The tone of one personality is hard like a horn; while the tone of another is soft like the high notes of a flute.

The gradual progress of all creation from a lower to a higher evolution; its change from one aspect to another; shows, as in transposition in music; the change of a melody from one key into another. The friendship and enmity among men, and their likes and dislikes, are as chords and discords. The harmony of human nature, and the human tendency to attraction and repulsion, is like the effect of the consonant and dissonant intervals in music.

In the tenderness of heart the tone turns into a half tone, and with the breaking of heart the tone breaks into microtones. The more tender the heart becomes, the fuller the tone becomes; the harder the heart grows, the more dead it sounds.

Each note, each scale and each strain expires at the appointed time, and at the end of the soul's experience here the finale comes, but the impression remains as the concert in a dream before the radiant vision of the consciousness.

With the music of the Absolute the bass, the undertone, is going on continuously, but on the surface and under the various keys of all the instruments of nature's music the undertone is hidden and subdued. Every being with life comes to the surface and again returns whence he came, as each note has its return to the ocean of sound. The undertone of this existence is the loudest and the softest, the highest and the lowest; it overwhelms all instruments of soft or loud, high or low tone, until all gradually merges in it; the undertone is always, and always will be.

The mystery of sound is called Mysticism; the harmony of life is Religion. The knowledge of vibrations is termed Metaphysics, and the analysis of atoms Science, and their harmonious grouping is Art. The rhythm of form is poetry, and the rhythm of sound is music. This shows that music is the art of arts and the science of all sciences, and it contains the fountain of all knowledge within itself.

Music is called a divine or celestial art, not only because of its use in religion and devotion, and because it is in itself an universal religion, but because of its fineness in comparison with all other arts and sciences. Every Sacred Scripture, Holy Picture or spoken word produces the impression of its identity upon the mirror of the soul, but music stands before the soul without producing any impression whatever of either name or form of this objective world thus preparing the soul to realize the Infinite.

The Sufi recognizing this names music *Giza-I-ruh*, the food of the soul and uses it as a source of spiritual perfection, for music fans the fire of the heart, and flame arising from it illumines the soul. The Sufi derives much more benefit from music in his meditations than from anything else. His devotional and meditative attitude makes him responsive to music which helps him in his spiritual unfoldment. The consciousness by the help of music first frees itself from the body and then from the mind. This, once accomplished, one step more only is needed to attain spiritual perfection.

Sufis in all have taken a keen interest in music in whatever land they may have dwelt; Rumi especially adopted this art by reason of his great devotion. He listened to the verses of the Mystics on love and truth sung by the *Kawals*, (the musicians), to the accompaniment of the flute.

The Sufi visualizes the object of his devotion in his mind which is reflected upon the mirror of his soul. The heart, the factor of feeling, is possessed by everyone, although with everyone it is not a living heart. This heart is made alive by the Sufi who gives an outlet to his intense feelings in tears and in sighs. By so doing the clouds of Jelal, the power which gathers with his psychic development, fall in tears as drops of rain, and the sky of his heart is clear, allowing the soul to shine. This condition is regarded by Sufis as the sacred ecstasy. Since the time of Rumi music has become a part of devotion in the Mevlavi Order of the Sufis. The masses in general, owing to their narrow orthodox views, have cast out the Sufis, and opposed them for their freedom of thought, misinterpreting the Prophet's teaching, who prohibited the *abuse* of music; not music; not music, in the real sense of the word. For this reason a language of music was made by Sufis, so that only the initiated could understand the meaning of the songs. Many in the East hear and enjoy these songs not understanding what they really mean.

A branch of this order come to India in ancient times, and was known as the Chisti School of Sufis; it was brought to great glory by Khaja Moinudin Chisti, one of the greatest Mystics ever known to the world. It would not be an exaggeration to say that he actually lived on music, and even in the present day, although his body has been in the tomb at Ajmere for many centuries, yet at his shrine there is always music performed by the best singers and musicians in the land. This shows the glory of a poverty-stricken Sage, compared with the poverty of a glorious king; the one during his life had all things, which ceased at his death, while with the Sage the glory is ever on the increase. At the present time music is prevalent in the school of the Chistis who hoid meditative musical assemblies called Suma or *Kawali*; during these they meditate on the ideal of their devotion which is in accordance with their grade of evolution, and they increase the fire of their devotion while listening to the music.

Wajad, the sacred ecstasy which the Sufis experience as a rule at Suma, may be said to be union with the Desired One. There are three aspects of this union which are experienced by Sufis of different stages of evolution. The first is the union with the revered Ideal from the plane of earth present before the devotee, either in the objective plane or in the plane of thought. The heart of the devotee, filled with love, admiration, and gratitude, then becomes capable of visualizing the form of his Ideal of devotion whilst listening to the music.

The second step in ecstasy, and the higher aspect of union, is union with the beauty of character of the Ideal irrespective of form.

The song in praise of the ideal character helps the love of the devotee to gush out and overflow. The third stage in ecstasy is union with the Divine Beloved, the highest Ideal, who is beyond the limitation of name and form, virtue or merit, with whom it has constantly sought union, and whom the soul has finally found. This joy is unexplainable. When the words of those souls who have already attained union with the Divine Beloved are sung before the one who is treading the path of divine love, he sees all the signs on the path described in those verses, and it is a great comfort to him. The praise of the One so idealized, so unlike the ideal of the world in general, fills him with joy beyond words.

Ecstasy, manifests in various aspects; sometimes a Sufi may be in tears; sometimes a sigh may manifest; sometimes it expresses itself in Rakhs; motion. All this is regarded

with respect and reverence by those present
at the Suma Assembly, as ecstasy is
considered to be divine bliss. The sighing of
the devotee clears a path for him into the world
unseen, and his tears wash away the sins of
ages. All revelation follows the ecstasy; all
knowledge that a book can never contain and
that a language can never express, or a
Teacher teach, comes to him of itself.

VIII

Abstract Sound

Abstract sound is called Saute Surmad by vibrations of this sound are too fine to be either audible or visible to the material ears or eyes, since it is even difficult for the eyes to see the form and color of the etherial vibrations on the external plane. It was the Saute Surmad, the sound of the abstract, which Mohammed heard in the cave of Gare-Hira when he became lost in his Divine Ideal; the Quran refers to this sound in the words "Be! and all became." Moses heard this very sound on Mount Sinai, when in Communion with God, and the same word was audible to the Christ when absorbed in his Heavenly Father in the wilderness. Shiva heard the same Anahad Nada during his Samadhi in the Cave of the Himalayas. The flute of Krishna is symbolic of the same sound allegorically

explained. This sound is the source of all
revelation to the Masters to whom it is
revealed from within; it is therefore that they
know and teach the one and the same Truth.
The Sufi knows of the past, present, and the
future, and about all things in life by being
able to know the direction of sound. Every
aspect of one's being in which sound manifests
has a peculiar effect upon life, for the activity
of vibrations has a special effect in every
direction. The knower of the mystery of sound
knows the mystery of the whole universe.
Whoever has followed the strains of this sound
has forgotten all earthly distinctions and
differences, and has reached the same goal or
Truth in which all the Blessed ones of God
unite. Space is within the body as well as
around it; in other words the body is in the
space and the space is in the body.

This being the case, the sound of the
abstract is always going on within, around and
about man. Man does not hear it as a rule,
because his consciousness is entirely centered
in his material existence. Man becomes so
absorbed in his experiences in the external
world through the medium of the physical
body that space, with all its wonders of light
and sound, appears to him blank. This can be
easily understood by studying the nature of
color. There are many colors that are quite
distinct by themselves, yet when mixed with
others of still brighter hue they become

altogether eclipsed; even bright colors embroidered with gold, silver, diamonds or pearls serve merely as a background to the dazzling embroidery. So it is with the abstract sound compared with the sounds of the external world. The limited volume of earthly sounds is so concrete, that it dims the effect of the sound of the Abstract to the sense of hearing, although in comparison to it the sounds of the earth are like that of a whistle to a drum. When the abstract sound is audible all other sounds become indistinct to the Mystic.

The sound of the Abstract is called Anahad in the Vedas, meaning unlimited sound. The Sufis name it *Surmad*, which suggests the idea of intoxication. The word intoxication is here used to signify upliftment; the freedom of the soul from its earthly bondage. Those who are able to hear the *Saute Surmad* and meditate on it are relieved from all worries, anxieties, sorrows, fears and diseases, and the soul is freed from captivity in the senses and in the physical body. The soul of the listener becomes the all-pervading consciousness; and his Spirit becomes the battery which keeps the whole universe in motion. Some train themselves to hear the *Saute Surmad* in the solitude on the sea shore, on the river bank, and in the hills and dales; others accomplish it while sitting in the caves of the mountains, or when wandering constantly through forests and deserts, keeping themselves in the wilderness apart from the haunts of men. Yogis and ascetics blow *Singh* (a horn) or *Shankha* (a shell) which awakens in them this inner tone. Dervishes play *Nai* or *Algoza* (a double flute) for the same purpose. The bells and gongs in the churches and temples are meant to suggest to the thinker the same sacred sound, and thus lead him toward the inner life. This sound develops through ten different aspects because of its manifestation through ten different tubes of the body; it sounds like thunder, the roaring of the sea, the jingling of bells, running water, the buzzing of bees, the twittering of sparrows, the Vina, the whistle, or the sound of *Shankha* until it finally becomes *Hu* the most sacred of all sounds. This sound Hu is the beginning and end of all sounds; be they from man, bird, beast, or thing. A minute study will prove this fact, which can be realized by listening to the sound of the steam engine or of a mill; the echo of bells or gongs give a typical illustration of the sound *Hu*.

The Supreme Being has been called by various names in different languages, but the Mystics have known him as *Hu* the natural name, not man made, the only name of the Nameless, which all nature constantly proclaims. The sound *Hu* is most sacred; the mystics of all ages called it *Ism-azam*, the name of the most High, for it is the origin and end of every sound as well as the background of each word. The word *Hu* is the spirit of all sounds and of all words, and is hidden under them all, as the spirit in the body. It does not belong to any language, but no language can help belonging to it. This alone is the true Name of God, a Name that no people and no religion can claim as their own. This word is not only uttered by human beings, but is repeated by animals and birds. All things and beings exclaim this name of the Lord, for every activity of life expresses distinctly or indistinctly this very sound. This is the word mentioned in the Bible as existing before the light came into being, "In the beginning was the Word, and the Word was with God, and the Word was God." (St. John i. I)

The mystery of *Hu* is revealed to the Sufi who journeys through the Path of Initiation. Truth, the knowledge of God, is termed by a Sufi *Hak*. If we divide the word *Hak* into two parts, it becomes *hu ak, Hu* signifying God, or Truth, and *ak* in Hindustani meaning one, both meanings together expressing one God and one Truth. *Hukikat* in Arabic means the essential truth, *Hakim* means master and *Hukim* means knower; all of which words express the essential characteristics of life.

Aluk is the sacred word that the Vairagis, the adepts of India, exclaim as their Sacred chant. In the word Aluk are expressed two words, al meaning from, and huk truth, both words together express God the source from which all comes.

The sound *Hu* becomes limited in the word *Hum*, for the letter *m* closes the lips. This word in Hindustani expresses limitation, *Hum* means I or We, both of which words signify ego. The word Humsa is the sacred word of the Yogis which illumines the ego with the light of reality. The word Huma in the Persian language stands for a fabulous bird. There is a belief that if the Huma Bird sits for a moment on the head of anybody it is a sign that the person will become a king. Its true explanation is, that when man's thoughts so evolve that they break all limitation he becomes as a king. It is the lack of language that it can only describe the Most High as something like a king. It is said in the old traditions that Zoroaster was born of a huma tree. This explains the words in the Bible, "Except a man be born of water and the Spirit, he cannot enter the Kingdom of God." In the word *huma, hu* represents spirit, and the word mah in Arabic means water. In English the word human explains two facts which are characteristic of humanity, *Hu* means God, *man* means mind, which word comes from Sanskrit mana, mind being the ordinary man; the two words united represent the idea of the God-conscious man, in other words *Hu*, God, is in all things and beings, but it is man by whom He is known Human therefore means God-conscious, God-realized, or God-man. The word *Humd* means praise, Humid, praiseworthy, and Mohumad, praiseful. The name of the Prophet of Islam was significant of his attitude to God.

Hur in Arabic means the beauties of the Heaven, its real meaning is the expressing of heavenly beauty. *Zhur* in Arabic means manifestation, especially that of God in nature.

Ahur Mazda is the name of God known to the Zoroastrians. In this first word *Ahur* suggests *hu* upon which the whole name is built. All of these examples signify the origin of God in the word *Hu*, and the life of God in everything and being.

Hai in Arabic means everlasting, and hai-yat means life, both of which words signify the everlasting nature of God. The word huwal suggests the idea of omni present, and huva is the origin of the name of Eve which is symbolic of manifestation: as Adam is symbolic of life, they are named in Sanskrit Purusha and Prakriti.

Jehovah is really *Yahuva* and originally was *Yahu, ya* denoting the word oh! And *Hu* standing for God, while the A represents manifestation. *Hu* is the origin of sound, but when the sound first takes shape on the external plane, it becomes A, therefore *alif* or *alpha* is considered to be the first expression of Hu, the original word. In Sanskrit as well as in all other languages A begins the alphabet as well as the name of God. The word A therefore expresses in English one or first, and the figure of alif gives the meaning one, as well as first. The letter A is pronounced without the help of the teeth or tongue, and in Sanskrit A always means without.

The A is raised to the surface when the tongue rises and touches the roof of the mouth when pronouncing the letter L (lam), and the sound ends in m (mim), the pronunciation of which closes the lips, therefore these three essential letters of the alphabet brought together as the mystery in the Koran form a word *alm*, which means knowledge. Alim comes from the same and means knower. Alam means state or condition; the existence which is known.

When alif the first and lam the central letters, are brought together they make the word al which means from in Arabic and may be interpreted to be "The latter derived from the former." In English "all" suggests the meaning of entire or absolute nature of existence.

The word Allah which in Arabic means God, if divided into three parts may be interpreted, "The one who comes from nothing." El or Ellah have the same meaning as Allah. The words found in the Bible Eloi, Elohim and Allelulia are a corruption of the word Allah-Hu.

The words om, omen, amen and ameen which are spoken in all houses of prayer are of the same origin; A in the commencement of the word expresses the beginning, and M in the midst signifies end, N the final letter being the re-echo of M, for M naturally ends in a nasal sound, the producing of which sound signifies life.

In the word, *Ahud*, which means God; the only Being; two meanings, are involved. A, in Sanskrit, means, without, and, hud, in Prakret, means limitation. The Persian, word, Khuda, has its origin in, huda, which signifies, "the limit and end of all things in Him."

It is from the same source, that the words, Wahadat, Wahadaniat, Hadi, Huda, and, Hidayat, all come.

Wahadat means, the consciousness, of self, alone; Wahadaniat, is the knowledge, of self; Hadi, the guide; Huda, the guide; Hidayat, means, guidance.

The more a Sufi listens to Saute Surmad, the sound of the Abstract, the more his consciousness becomes free from all the limitations of life. The soul floats above the physical and mental plane without any special effort on man's part, which shows its calm and peaceful state; a dreamy look comes into calm and peaceful state; a dreamy look comes into his eyes and his countenance becomes radiant, he experiences the unearthly joy and rapture of Wajad (Ecstasy). When Ecstasy overwhelms

him he is neither conscious of the physical
existence nor of the mental. This is the
Heavenly Wine, to which all Sufi Poets refer,
and is totally unlike the momentary
intoxications of this mortal plane. A heavenly
bliss then springs in the heart of a Sufi, his
mind is purified from sin, his body from all
impurities, and a pathway is opened for him
toward the world unseen; he begins to receive
inspirations, intuitions, impressions, and
revelations without the least effort on his part.
He is no longer dependent upon a Book or a
Teacher, for divine wisdom, the light of his
soul, the Holy Spirit, begins to shine upon him.

"I by the light of Soul realize that the
beauty of the Heavens and the grandeur of
the earth are the echo of Thy magic Flute"
(Sherif).

Other Titles in this Series
BY PILGRIMS PUBLISHING

For Catalog & More Information, Write To:
PILGRIMS BOOK HOUSE
P.O Box: 3872, Thamel
Kathmandu, Nepal
Tel: 977-1- 424942, 425919
Fax: 977-1- 424943
Email: pilgrims@wlink.com.np
Website: www.pilgrimsbooks.com